BACTERIA UP CLOSE

UNDER THE
MICROSCOPE

Gareth Stevens
Publishing

BY GREG ROZA

Please visit our website, www.garethstevens.com. For a free color catalog of all our high-quality books, call toll free 1-800-542-2595 or fax 1-877-542-2596.

Library of Congress Cataloging-in-Publication Data

Roza, Greg.
Bacteria up close / Greg Roza.
    pages cm. — (Under the microscope)
Includes bibliographical references and index.
ISBN 978-1-4339-8335-1 (pbk.)
ISBN 978-1-4339-8336-8 (6-pack)
ISBN 978-1-4339-8334-4 (library binding)
1. Bacteria—Juvenile literature. 2. Microscopy—Juvenile literature. 3. Medical microbiology—Juvenile literature. I. Title.
QR74.8.R69 2014
616.9'041—dc23

                         2012047096

First Edition

Published in 2014 by
Gareth Stevens Publishing
111 East 14th Street, Suite 349
New York, NY 10003

Copyright © 2014 Gareth Stevens Publishing

Designer: Katelyn E. Reynolds
Editor: Therese Shea

Photo credits: Cover, p. 1 J. L. Carson/Custom Medical Stock Photo/Getty Images; cover, pp. 1, 3–31 (logo and bacteria image icons) iStockphoto/Thinkstock.com; cover, pp. 1–31 (bacteria image icon) Ingram Publishing/Thinkstock.com; cover, pp. 1–32 (background texture) Hemera/Thinkstock.com; p. 5 Jupiterimages/Goodshot/Thinkstock.com; p. 7 NYPL/ Science Source/Photo Researchers/Getty Images; p. 8 Keystone Features/Getty Images; p. 9 Rischgitz/Getty Images; pp. 10, 15, 19 Dorling Kindersley RF/Thinkstock.com; p. 11 Scott Camazine/Photo Researchers/Getty Images; p. 12 Visuals Unlimited, Inc./Carol & Mike Werner/Getty Images; pp. 13, 17 LadyofHats/Wikipedia.com; p. 14 CNRI/Science Photo Library/Getty Images; p. 16 Morgan/Science Source – Hank/Photo Researchers/ Getty Images; p. 20 CMSP/Custom Medical Stock Photo/Getty Images; p. 21 Visuals Unlimited, Inc./Nigel Cattlin/Getty Images; p. 23 Photo Researchers/Getty Images; p. 24 Science Photo Library/Getty Images; p. 25 Visuals Unlimited, Inc./Scientifica/RMF/Getty Images; p. 27 Aubord Dulac/Shutterstock.com; p. 29 Fernan Federici/Flickr/Getty Images.

Printed in the United States of America

CPSIA compliance information: Batch #CS13GS: For further information contact Gareth Stevens, New York, New York at 1-800-542-2595.

CONTENTS

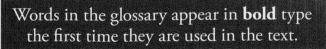

Words in the glossary appear in **bold** type the first time they are used in the text.

WHAT ARE THEY?

DID YOU KNOW?

You might be surprised to learn that billions of bacteria are living on and inside you right now!

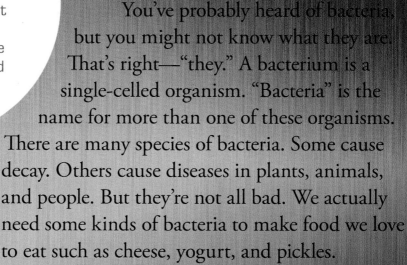

You've probably heard of bacteria, but you might not know what they are. That's right—"they." A bacterium is a single-celled organism. "Bacteria" is the name for more than one of these organisms. There are many species of bacteria. Some cause decay. Others cause diseases in plants, animals, and people. But they're not all bad. We actually need some kinds of bacteria to make food we love to eat such as cheese, yogurt, and pickles.

It's a good thing bacteria aren't all bad, because they're everywhere! They're just too small to see without a microscope. In fact, before microscopes, people didn't know bacteria existed. They weren't discovered until the late 1600s. As microscopes have developed over the years, we've been able to see the many shapes and sizes of these incredible organisms.

INVENTING
MICROSCOPES

Microscopes have been used to make numerous scientific discoveries. The first microscope was made in 1590 when Dutch lens makers put two lenses inside a tube. Scientists, including Galileo Galilei, experimented with lenses and made great improvements to microscopes. While the first microscope could only magnify objects about 10 times, the most powerful microscopes today can magnify objects up to 20 million times! This magnification is enough to let scientists see the atoms that make up matter.

Bacteria vary in shape and size, but all are very, very small.

THE HISTORY OF BACTERIA

DID YOU KNOW?

When he was a teen, van Leeuwenhoek worked for a fabric maker. He used magnifying lenses to check thread counts. This was van Leeuwenhoek's first experience with lenses.

Microbiology and the study of bacteria began with Dutch scientist Antonie van Leeuwenhoek (LAY-vehn-hook). During the 1660s, van Leeuwenhoek became interested in making lenses as a hobby. His first microscopes were nothing more than very powerful magnifying lenses. Van Leeuwenhoek magnified many things with his microscopes, including pond scum, rainwater, and well water. He was shocked to find tiny creatures living in these and other sources—including his own mouth! Van Leeuwenhoek had discovered bacteria. Today, thanks to this and several other scientific contributions, van Leeuwenhoek is considered the father of microbiology.

Van Leeuwenhoek's discoveries inspired many other scientists to follow in his footsteps. German scientist Christian Gottfried Ehrenberg studied microscopic fossils. Ehrenberg came up with the name "bacterium" in 1838 to describe some microscopic creatures.

WHAT IS
MICROBIOLOGY?

Microbiology is the study of creatures so small we need a microscope to see them. These include bacteria, fungi, viruses, and other organisms. Microbiologists study microscopic organisms—or microorganisms—to determine how they affect people and the **environment**. Microbiologists have made advancements in many areas of science. They've even helped us understand the microorganisms responsible for some of the foods we eat as well as microorganisms that make us sick, which we call "germs."

Van Leeuwenhoek's microscopes could magnify objects by about 200 times.

CLEAN YOUR LAB,
MR. FLEMING!

Antibiotics are drugs that kill harmful bacteria. The first antibiotic was found by accident! Scottish scientist Alexander Fleming was studying harmful bacteria. While cleaning his laboratory one day in 1928, Fleming noticed mold growing in a glass dish. He was shocked to find that the mold had killed the bacteria that had been in the dish. This discovery led to the development of penicillin, which is an antibiotic still widely used to treat bacterial **infections**.

Alexander Fleming won the 1945 Nobel Prize in Medicine for his work with penicillin.

In the mid-1800s, French chemistry professor Louis Pasteur helped solve a problem at a local business that made alcohol. During his studies, Pasteur discovered that microorganisms—yeast and mold—are responsible for the process that creates beer and wine, called **fermentation**. He also showed that bacteria caused these alcohols to spoil. This discovery was big news for the makers of beer and wine, but it also led to a new scientific idea: the germ theory of disease.

Pasteur discovered that many diseases, including **cholera** and **smallpox**, were caused by microorganisms. He recommended **vaccinations** to prevent the spread of diseases like these. Pasteur also developed a process of heating alcohol to kill the bacteria in it and keep it from spoiling. Today, the "pasteurization" process is widely used to keep milk from spoiling.

DID YOU KNOW?

The findings of Pasteur and other scientists disproved an age-old theory that living things developed from nonliving things—a theory called spontaneous generation.

Louis Pasteur in his laboratory

9

GETTING TO KNOW BACTERIA

Since Fleming discovered penicillin, great strides have been made in bacteriology, or the study of bacteria. Scientists have learned a lot about harmful bacteria and how to combat them. However, they've also discovered that many bacteria are actually helpful to people.

Bacteria are single-celled organisms. Many are just 1 micrometer, or micron, long—that's just one-millionth of a meter! Some are smaller, and some are larger. Bacteria come in three main shapes. They can be round or oval shaped, rod shaped, or **spiral** shaped. Most, but not all, bacteria are capable of movement. Some use narrow, whiplike parts called flagella. Some can spin and turn. Others make a slime to glide around, somewhat like snails.

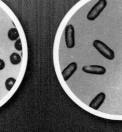

oval

rod

spiral

PROKARYOTES

Bacteria are prokaryotes. They're different from human cells, which are called eukaryotes. Like human cells, prokaryotes have an outer **membrane** that protects their insides. Unlike human cells, however, prokaryotes' tiny organs, or organelles, aren't surrounded by membranes. Instead, they float in a liquid called cytoplasm within the cell. Prokaryotes are the most common forms of life on Earth, and most are bacteria.

This is a microscopic image of the spiral-shaped bacterium that causes Lyme disease. It's transmitted to people through tick bites.

WHAT ARE GENES?

All living cells have genetic material, or DNA. Genes are bits of DNA that determine the **traits** that parents pass on to their offspring. In human cells, there are genes for hair color, eye color, freckles, height, and many other physical traits. DNA is packed in thread-like structures called chromosomes. In human cells, chromosomes are in the nucleus, which is somewhat like a cell's brain. In bacteria, chromosomes float freely in the nucleoid.

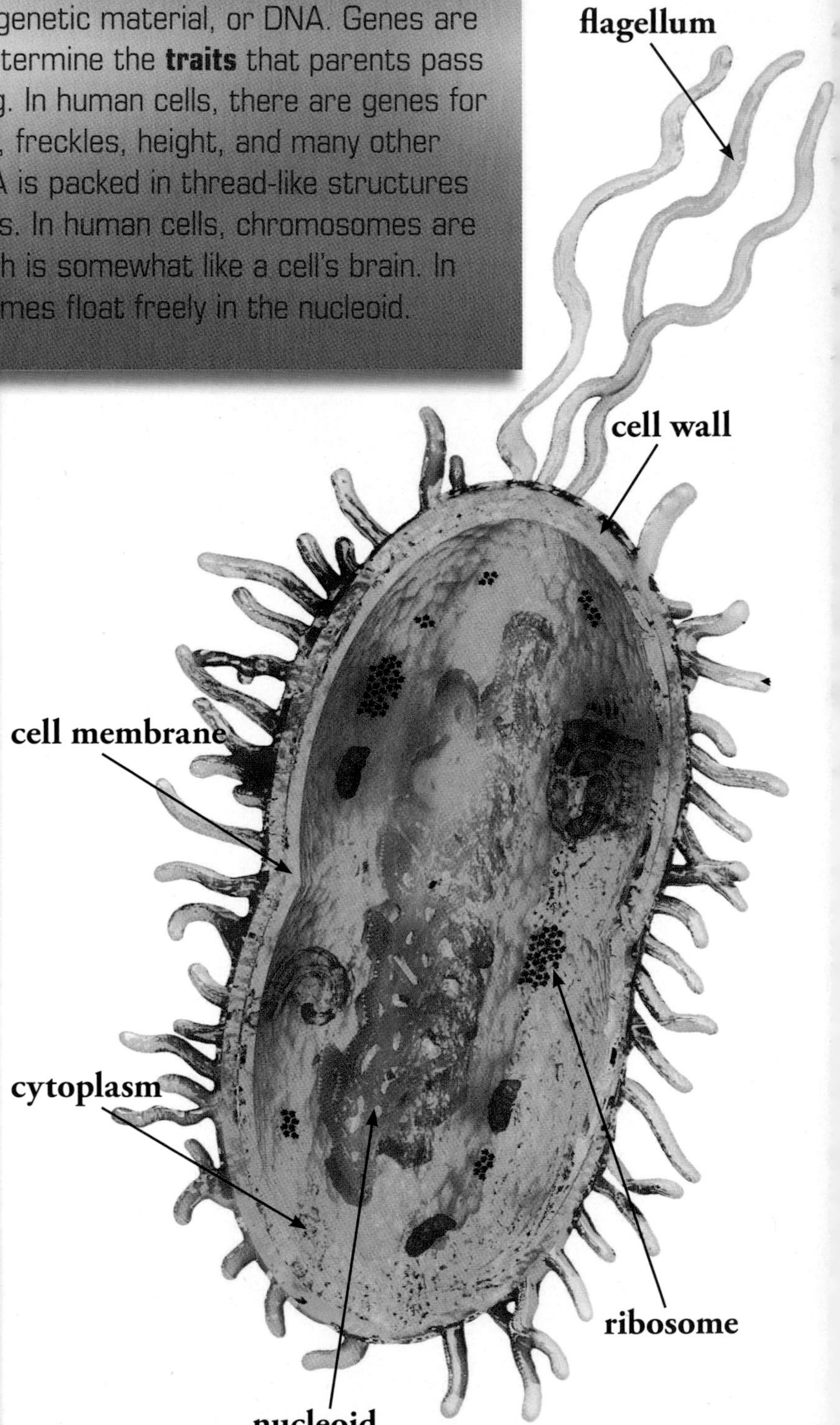

flagellum

cell wall

cell membrane

This picture shows some basic parts of a bacterium. Not all bacteria have cell walls or flagella.

cytoplasm

ribosome

nucleoid

Most bacteria are surrounded by an outer cell wall that protects them from their surroundings. Inside the cell wall is the cell membrane, which stops harmful chemicals from entering the cell. Inside the cell membrane, the bacterium's organelles float freely in cytoplasm. The cytoplasm also holds important **enzymes** that help break down food and build cell parts.

The cells of many living creatures have a nucleus surrounded by a membrane. This holds a cell's genetic material. Bacteria, however, don't have a nucleus. Their genetic material floats freely in an area of the cell called the nucleoid. This genetic material controls all activity in the cell, including growth and reproduction. A bacterium also has stored **nutrients** and ribosomes. Ribosomes create the proteins needed for growth, repair, and other biological processes.

DID YOU KNOW?

Scientists believe that bacteria were among the first forms of life on Earth. Fossil records show that they first appeared about 3.5 billion years ago.

SO MANY BACTERIA!

Bacteria reproduce very easily and very quickly. In fact, one species can double its numbers in just 20 minutes. If a single bacterium is given enough food, it can create a billion more cells just like itself through binary fission in just 10 hours! The ability to reproduce rapidly has helped bacteria survive and flourish for billions of years. In fact, this trait makes some harmful bacteria incredibly difficult to fight.

This image of an *E. coli* bacterium shows the organism in the early stages of binary fission. You can see the cell membrane growing through the middle of the cell.

Most bacteria can reproduce by themselves. Usually, a single bacterium splits into two new cells. This process is called binary fission. "Binary" means "having two parts." "Fission" is the act of splitting into different parts. When a bacterium undergoes binary fission, it grows to about twice its normal size. It makes an exact copy of its DNA. The cell membrane then grows down the middle of the cell, and each side gets its own genetic material.

Some bacteria reproduce through a process called budding. This occurs when a new cell, called a "daughter," grows on the side of a parent cell, called a "mother." The mother creates genetic material for the daughter. The daughter grows larger and separates from the mother, resulting in a new cell.

DID YOU KNOW?

Some bacteria share DNA with each other through a process called conjugation. The bacteria gain traits that help them adapt to different environments.

binary fission   budding

NAME GAME

The names scientists give to different kinds of bacteria are based on their shape and the way they group together. Round bacteria are called cocci, rod-shaped bacteria are called bacilli, and spiral bacteria are called spirilla. Prefixes are used to describe bacteria joined together in groups. *Diplo-* describes a pair of bacteria. Bacteria in a cluster have the prefix *staphylo-*, and chains of bacteria have the prefix *strepto-*.

These are streptococcus bacteria, which cause pneumonia. The round bacteria are organized in chains.

With bacteria's ability to multiply so quickly, it's probably not surprising to hear that most live in large groups known as colonies. Colonies can take on different forms depending on the species. Many group closely together in clusters. Others form long chains.

The substance in or on which a bacteria colony grows is called the growth medium. The more food available in the growth medium, the faster the colony will grow. As food sources decrease, so does the size of the colony. The largest known bacteria colonies are found in Earth's oceans. In 2010, scientists discovered a giant "mat" of bacteria in the Pacific Ocean off the coast of South America. This colony covers about the same amount of space as the country Greece!

DID YOU KNOW?

When a bacteria colony is cultivated, or grown, in a laboratory, it's called a culture.

diplococci

staphylococci

streptobacilli

THEY'RE EVERYWHERE!

DID YOU KNOW?

Scientists have discovered that a species of bacteria is "eating" the oil from the Deepwater Horizon oil rig disaster that occurred in the Gulf of Mexico in 2010.

Bacteria are found everywhere on Earth's surface. They can survive in the frozen polar ice caps and in the near-boiling water of hot springs. Some live around volcanic vents on the ocean floor. Bacteria live quite comfortably on and inside plants and animals. They live on tables, chairs, floors, sinks, and many other objects in homes. Many kinds of bacteria even live in the air we breathe.

In order to survive, bacteria need a source of food. Some bacteria make food the same way plants do—with sunlight, carbon dioxide, and water. Other bacteria make enzymes and use them to break down outside matter into nutrients small enough to pass through their cell wall. Some even consume inorganic materials, such as sulfur and iron.

WITH OR WITHOUT
OXYGEN?

Aerobes are microorganisms that "breathe" oxygen and use it for growth and energy. Some microorganisms, called anaerobes, don't need oxygen. They break down organic matter into simpler matter, which is then used for growth and energy. Oxygen stops some anaerobes from growing, or it kills them. Some bacteria are both aerobes and anaerobes. They use oxygen when it's available and switch to fermentation when there's no oxygen.

Bacteria love the moist and food-rich environment of people's mouths. That's why it's important to brush your teeth.

LIVING WITH
LEGUMES

Rhizobia are bacteria that change **nitrogen** in the air into compounds that plants use. They form a special partnership with some kinds of plants, particularly legumes such as peanuts and beans. Rhizobia live in bumps that form on the roots of legumes. The legumes make substances that help the bacteria grow, and the bacteria provide the legumes with a usable form of nitrogen.

When two species live together and help each other survive, they're said to share a "symbiotic" relationship. This close-up photo shows rhizobia living in legume roots.

One place you can find a lot of bacteria is in soil. The bacteria in soil are essential decomposers. A decomposer is an organism that helps break down dead plants and animals, causing them to decay. When bacteria feed on dead organisms, they release the nutrients locked in the organisms and return them to the soil. Then, plants use the nutrients for growth and energy. Some bacteria can break down even the hardest of organic material, such as chitin, which makes up the shells of many animals.

Several bacteria species help sustain life on Earth by changing nitrogen in the air into forms plants can use. Some bacteria help join nitrogen with other elements to form compounds plants can use, such as ammonia.

DID YOU KNOW?

A single teaspoon of healthy soil can contain between 100 million and 1 billion bacteria.

rhizobia lumps on the roots of a bean plant

HELPFUL OR HARMFUL?

DID YOU KNOW?

Sewage treatment plants use bacteria to help break down solid waste in wastewater.

Bacteria interact with other organisms in many ways. Many of these interactions are very helpful to us. You've already learned how bacteria in the soil can help plants get the nitrogen they need, which is good for farmers and gardeners, as well as anyone who enjoys a nice salad! Bacteria also help recycle other elements in our world, including carbon and sulfur.

Some bacteria are added to food products to change sugars to a substance called lactic acid through fermentation. Lactic acid thickens and flavors milk, which is then used to make cheese and yogurt. Some yogurts in stores contain live bacteria. These "active cultures" are believed to help the body fight harmful bacteria and aid **digestion**. Bacteria are also used to make sour cream, sausage, pickles, olives, and sauerkraut.

SO HAPPY
TOGETHER

Human intestines are home to millions of bacteria! While that might sound gross, those bacteria are very helpful to people. Intestinal bacteria break down compounds the human body can't, helping us digest our food. They also produce vitamins the body needs. Intestinal bacteria kill harmful microorganisms before they can make us sick. In return, we provide the bacteria with a plentiful source of food.

Helpful live microorganisms are sometimes called probiotics. These bacteria are found in probiotic yogurt.

"FLESH EATING" BACTERIA

Perhaps the scariest bacterial infection is necrotizing fasciitis (death of the fascia, or layers of tissue). Several different kinds of bacteria cause this disease. They're commonly known as "flesh eating" bacteria. The bacteria usually enter the body through a wound and then reproduce rapidly. They make a toxin that destroys tissue very quickly. While rare, necrotizing fasciitis is fatal in 30 to 40 percent of all cases. Victims who live are often left scarred or disabled.

Harmful microorganisms, such as the bacteria that cause disease, are called pathogens. These bacteria were found on human white blood cells.

While most bacteria are harmless or even helpful, some can make people sick. Some even kill. Harmful bacteria in air, water, and food can enter our body. We can also come into contact with harmful bacteria through sick people and the objects they've touched. Illnesses caused by bacteria range from mild food poisoning to deadly cholera.

Bacteria, commonly called germs, may cause infections when they get inside the body. Some bacteria produce harmful substances called toxins that cause diseases. Toxins can be made by living bacteria or can be released when bacteria die. Some bacteria normally found in the body can cause illnesses when they reproduce more quickly than the body can fight them off. Other species harm plants and animals on farms where we get our food.

DID YOU KNOW?

Cholera bacteria are spread though the solid waste of people who are sick with the disease. Each year, over 100,000 people around the world die from cholera.

cholera bacteria

FIGHTING BACTERIA

DID YOU KNOW?

A harmful microorganism that causes the immune system to respond to a threat is called an antigen.

People have an immune system that knows how to fight harmful bacteria. The immune system is made up of cells, tissues, and organs that work together to battle pathogens. When harmful bacteria enter the body, white blood cells work to destroy them. White blood cells produce substances called antibodies, which identify and bind to germs. An antibody that binds to a toxin is called an antitoxin. Once this occurs, other white blood cells called T cells destroy the harmful bacteria.

Sometimes our immune system needs help battling harmful bacteria. That's when antibiotics are needed. These drugs contain substances made by microorganisms that can kill harmful bacteria. Some antibiotics contain antitoxins from animal bodies. Some chemicals, such as antiseptics and disinfectants, can also kill bacteria or stop their growth.

HOW VACCINES WORK

A vaccine is a drug made from antigens that are weak or dead. When a vaccine is introduced into the body, the immune system creates specific antibodies to attack and kill the antigens. Once the immune system has destroyed the antigens, it stores the antibodies for future use. If someone who has received a vaccine later comes in contact with the same antigens, the body will be ready to fight it off.

One of the most effective ways of battling harmful bacteria is by washing your hands several times throughout the day.

27

AMAZING MICROORGANISMS

Ever since van Leeuwenhoek first spied the tiny organisms that live nearly everywhere in our world, scientists have been trying to learn more about bacteria. They've discovered many fascinating facts. Scientists recently found a species of bacteria eating plastic waste floating in the North Atlantic Ocean. They're currently studying the bacteria to see if they could be helpful in ridding the planet of excess plastic garbage. They aren't sure if the bacteria produce harmful toxins when they break down plastic. They also wonder how the plastic-eating bacteria have affected wildlife in the area.

Whether they're eating plastic, making cheese, or helping us digest our food, bacteria are some of the most interesting creatures on the planet!

GLOWING BACTERIA!

Bioluminescence is the ability of a living organism to produce light. Fireflies have this ability. Some kinds of bacteria do, too. The deep-sea anglerfish has a glowing lure that dangles in front of a mouthful of sharp teeth. The anglerfish can thank glowing bacteria that live in this amazing feature. Other bacteria glow because they want to be noticed—and eaten—by fish. Once eaten, they receive a never-ending source of food. As they grow in number, they may cause the fish to glow, too!

These beakers contain light-producing bacteria.

GLOSSARY

cholera: a bacterial disease of the intestines

digestion: the process of breaking down food so the body can use it

environment: the natural world in which a plant or animal lives

enzyme: a protein made in the body that helps chemical reactions occur

fermentation: a process by which an organism changes a sugar or starch into an alcohol or acid in the absence of oxygen

infection: a sickness caused by germs

membrane: a thin tissue in the body

nitrogen: a colorless, odorless gas that plays an important role in the health of plants

nutrient: something a living thing needs to grow and stay alive

smallpox: an illness caused by a microorganism called a virus

spiral: a shape or line that curls outward from a center point

trait: a feature, such as hair color, that is passed on from parents to children

vaccination: the injection of weakened or dead microorganisms to build up the immune system against a disease

FOR MORE INFORMATION

BOOKS

Biskup, Agnieszka. *The Surprising World of Bacteria with Max Axiom, Super Scientist*. Mankato, MN: Capstone Press, 2010.

Parker, Steve. *Cocci, Spirilla & Other Bacteria*. Minneapolis, MN: Compass Point Books, 2009.

Weakland, Mark. *Gut Bugs, Dust Mites, and Other Microorganisms You Can't Live Without*. Mankato, MN: Capstone Press, 2011.

WEBSITES

Bacteria
science.howstuffworks.com/environmental/life/cellular-microscopic/bacteria-info.htm
Read more about the microscopic world of bacteria.

What Are Germs?
kidshealth.org/kid/talk/qa/germs.html
Learn more about the microorganisms that cause illnesses, including bacteria.

INDEX